perfect ro[illegible]s

Essential dishes for everyday cooking

LOVE FOOD

Love Food ® is an imprint of Parragon Books Ltd

Parragon
Queen Street House
4 Queen Street
Bath BA1 1HE, UK

ISBN: 978-1-4075-3405-3

Printed in China

Designed by Talking Design
Cover text and introduction by Frances Eames

Notes for the reader

This book uses both metric and imperial measurements. Follow the same units of measurement throughout; do not mix metric with imperial. All spoon measurements are level, unless otherwise stated: teaspoons are assumed to be 5 ml and tablespoons are assumed to be 15 ml. Unless otherwise stated, milk is assumed to be semi-skimmed, eggs and individual vegetables such as potatoes are medium, and pepper is freshly ground black pepper. Recipes using raw or very lightly cooked eggs should be avoided by infants, the elderly, pregnant women, convalescents and anyone suffering from an illness. The times given are an approximate guide only.

Contents

introduction

Roasting is easy and produces delicious results. It is an effort-free method of cooking, as the work is done by the oven while you put your feet up. You may not have realised what a variety roasting offers, but it really can refresh your culinary repertoire. From Roast Chicken Breasts with Sun-blush Tomato Pesto to Roast Monkfish with Romesco Sauce, this book will open your eyes to the possibility of roasting delicious meals every day.

In an age of pre-prepared meals for one, roasting provides nutritious and convenient home cooking. Roasting is not just for cold winter nights, but, with dishes that emphasise colour, freshness and taste, is also perfect for the longer, lighter evenings. Try Fish Roasted with Lime accompanied by Roast Summer Vegetables for a zesty meal – perfect with a glass of chilled white wine.

The most famous roasted dish, the Sunday roast, has been traced back to Yorkshire, England, during the Industrial Revolution. It is believed this tradition arose because the meat could be put in the oven to cook before church on a Sunday morning. When the family arrived home at lunchtime, a delicious meal would be waiting. Now, however, the roast has been used for all manner of foods; roast meats, poultry, fish and a whole host of vegetable delights. It is a modern, convenient and versatile method of cooking.

True variety

Roast dinners offer great variety and flexibility. Roasting produces some of the best culinary results and keeps meat, fish and poultry tender and moist.

- Meat – You can use beef, lamb or pork. Think rich sauces such as Roast Venison with Brandy Sauce or melt in the mouth meat with recipes such as Slow Roast Pork. Beef can be well cooked or served slightly rare. Lamb shoulders or shanks roast very well and other meats, like ham, add a different dimension to a meal.

- Poultry – Chicken is one of the most popular birds for roasting, but this book will also show you recipes for turkey, duck and goose. Turkey, of course, is one roast that you will recognise. Take a look at Turkey with Bread Sauce for a family gathering. Tasty dishes such as Roast Duck Breasts with Onion Marmalade bring restaurant cuisine into your home.

- Fish – Now you can begin to see the possibilities of perfect fish roasting! You can roast a variety of fish, and this book looks at salmon, monkfish, haddock, cod and seafood. For a Mediterranean flavour, try Italian Cod, or for an intense texture and taste, try Garlic-Crusted Roast Haddock.

- Vegetables – Roasted vegetables are a true delight. They can form the main part of the meal, proving that vegetarian menus really do rival meat-based ones. Alternatively, the vegetable recipes in this book can serve as accompaniment dishes to meat, poultry or fish roasts. Lemon Butter Leeks with Poor Man's Parmesan provide delicious, simple fare; or try a twist on tradition with Chilli Roast Potatoes. If you wish to increase your vegetable consumption, what better way than with some of these innovative vegetable meals.

Equipment

Roasting really is an easy method of cooking. Unlike some complicated recipes involving every pot and pan in the kitchen, equipment for roasting can be minimal. If you use an attractive ceramic roasting dish for cooking, you can take this to the table for people to serve themselves. This cuts down the number of dishes you will need to wash. If you're a novice chef you will need to make sure you have the following equipment:

- Heavy-based saucepan
- Flameproof casserole dishes
- Chopping board and knives
- Peeler
- Large plates
- Slotted spoon and serving spoon/ladle
- Foil
- Serving dishes – warmed

mighty **meat**

Roast
Beef

SERVES 8

1 prime rib of beef, weighing 2.7 kg/ 6 lb
2 tsp English mustard powder
3 tbsp plain flour
300 ml/10 fl oz full-bodied red wine
300 ml/10 fl oz beef stock
2 tsp Worcestershire sauce (optional)
salt and pepper

Preheat the oven to 230°C/450°F/Gas Mark 8. Season the meat to taste with salt and pepper and rub in the mustard and 1 tablespoon of the flour.

Put the meat in a roasting tin large enough to hold it comfortably and roast in the preheated oven for 15 minutes. Reduce the heat to 190°C/375°F/Gas Mark 5 and cook for 1 hour 45 minutes for rare beef or 2 hours 20 minutes for medium beef. Baste the meat occasionally to keep it moist. If the tin becomes too dry, add a little red wine or stock.

When the meat is cooked, transfer to a warmed serving plate, cover loosely with foil and leave to rest for 10–15 minutes.

To make the gravy, pour off most of the fat from the roasting tin, then put the tin over a medium heat and scrape the sediment from the base. Sprinkle in the remaining flour and quickly whisk it into the juices. When you have a smooth paste, gradually add the wine and most of the stock, whisking constantly. Bring to the boil, then reduce the heat and cook for 2–3 minutes until thickened. Season to taste with salt and pepper, add the remaining stock, if necessary, and a little Worcestershire sauce, if you like.

When ready to serve, carve the meat into slices and serve on warmed plates. Pour the gravy into a warmed jug to serve.

beef pot roast with *Potatoes*

SERVES 6

2½ tbsp plain flour
1 tsp salt
¼ tsp pepper
1 rolled brisket joint, weighing 1.6 kg/3 lb 8 oz
2 tbsp vegetable oil
2 tbsp butter
1 onion, finely chopped
2 celery sticks, diced
2 carrots, diced
1 tsp dill seed
1 tsp dried thyme or oregano
350 ml/12 fl oz full-bodied red wine
150–225 ml/5–8 fl oz beef stock
4–5 potatoes, cut into large chunks and boiled until just tender
2 tbsp chopped fresh dill, to garnish

Preheat the oven to 140°C/275°F/Gas Mark 1. Mix 2 tablespoons of the flour with the salt and pepper in a shallow dish. Dip the meat into the mixture to coat. Heat the oil in a flameproof casserole. Add the brisket and cook until browned all over. Transfer to a plate.

Melt half the butter in the casserole over a medium heat. Add the onion, celery, carrots, dill seed and thyme and cook, stirring frequently, for 5 minutes. Return the meat and juices to the casserole.

Pour in the wine and enough stock to reach one third of the way up the meat. Bring to the boil, then reduce the heat, cover and cook in the preheated oven for 3 hours, turning the meat every 30 minutes. After the meat has been cooking for 2 hours, add the potatoes and more stock, if necessary.

When ready, transfer the meat and vegetables to a warmed serving dish. Sieve the cooking liquid into a saucepan.

Mix the remaining butter and flour to a paste. Bring the cooking liquid to the boil. Whisk in small pieces of the flour and butter paste, whisking constantly until the sauce is smooth. Pour the sauce over the meat and vegetables. Sprinkle with the fresh dill and serve immediately.

Slow
Roast Pork

SERVES 6

- 1 piece of loin of pork, weighing 1.6 kg/3 lb 8 oz, boned and rolled
- 4 garlic cloves, thinly sliced lengthways
- 1½ tsp finely chopped fennel fronds or ⅓ tsp dried fennel
- 4 cloves
- 300 ml/10 fl oz dry white wine
- 300 ml/10 fl oz water
- salt and pepper

Preheat the oven to 150°C/300°F/Gas Mark 2.

Use a small, sharp knife to make incisions all over the pork, opening them out slightly to make little pockets. Place the garlic slices in a small sieve and rinse under cold running water to moisten.

Spread out the fennel on a saucer and roll the garlic slices in it to coat. Slide the garlic slices and the cloves into the pockets in the pork. Season the meat all over to taste with salt and pepper. Place the pork in a large ovenproof dish or roasting tin. Pour in the wine and water. Cook in the oven, basting the meat occasionally, for 2½–2¾ hours, until the pork is tender but still quite moist.

If you are serving the pork hot, transfer it to a carving board, cover with foil and leave to rest before cutting it into slices. If you are serving it cold, leave it to cool completely in the cooking juices before removing and slicing.

Roast Pork
with crackling

SERVES 4

- 1 kg/2 lb 4 oz piece of pork loin, boned and the skin removed and reserved
- 2 tbsp mustard
- salt and pepper
- apple sauce , to serve

Gravy

- 1 tbsp flour
- 300 ml/10 fl oz cider, apple juice or stock
- salt and pepper

Preheat the oven to 200°C/400°F/Gas Mark 6.

Make sure the skin of the pork is well scored and sprinkle with salt. Place on a wire rack on a baking tray and roast for 30–40 minutes until the crackling is golden brown and crispy. This can be cooked in advance, leaving room in the oven for roast potatoes.

Season the loin of pork well with salt and pepper and spread the fat with the mustard. Place in a roasting tin and roast in the centre of the oven for 20 minutes. Reduce the oven temperature to 190°C/375°F/Gas Mark 5 and cook for 50–60 minutes until the meat is a good colour and the juices run clear when the meat is pierced with a skewer.

Remove the meat from the oven and place on a hot serving plate, cover with foil and leave in a warm place.

To make the gravy, pour off most of the fat from the roasting tin, leaving the meat juices and the sediments. Sprinkle in the flour, whisking well. Cook the paste for a couple of minutes, then add the cider a little at a time until you have a smooth gravy. Boil for 2–3 minutes until it is the required consistency. Season well with salt and pepper and pour into a hot serving jug. Carve the pork into slices and serve on hot plates with pieces of the crackling and the gravy. Serve with apple sauce.

Roast
Ham

SERVES 6

1 boneless gammon joint, weighing 1.3 kg/3 lb, pre-soaked if necessary
2 tbsp Dijon mustard
85 g/3 oz demerara sugar
½ tsp ground cinnamon
½ tsp ground ginger
18 whole cloves

Cumberland Sauce

2 Seville oranges, halved
4 tbsp redcurrant jelly
4 tbsp port
1 tsp mustard
salt and pepper

Place the joint in a large saucepan, cover with cold water and gradually bring to the boil over a low heat. Cover and simmer very gently for 1 hour. Preheat the oven to 200°C/400°F/Gas Mark 6. Meanwhile, make the Cumberland Sauce. Using a zester, remove the zest from the oranges and reserve. Place the redcurrant jelly, port and mustard in a small saucepan and heat gently until the jelly has melted. Squeeze the juice from the oranges into the saucepan. Add the orange zest and season to taste with salt and pepper. Serve cold with gammon. The sauce can be kept in a screw-top jar in the refrigerator for up to 2 weeks.

Remove the gammon from the saucepan and drain. Remove the rind from the gammon and discard. Score the fat into a diamond-shaped pattern with a sharp knife. Spread the mustard over the fat. Mix the sugar and ground spices together on a plate and roll the gammon in it, pressing down to coat evenly.

Stud the diamond shapes with cloves and place the joint in a roasting tin. Roast in the oven for 20 minutes until the glaze is a rich golden colour.

To serve hot, cover with foil and leave to stand for 20 minutes before carving. If the gammon is to be served cold, it can be cooked a day ahead. Serve with the Cumberland Sauce.

Rack
of Lamb

SERVES 2

1 trimmed rack of lamb, weighing 250–300 g/9–10½ oz
1 garlic clove, crushed
150 ml/5 fl oz red wine
1 fresh rosemary sprig, crushed to release the flavour
1 tbsp olive oil
150 ml/5 fl oz lamb stock
2 tbsp redcurrant jelly
salt and pepper

Mint Sauce

Bunch fresh mint leaves
2 tsp caster sugar
2 tbsp boiling water
2 tbsp white wine vinegar

Place the rack of lamb in a non-metallic bowl and rub all over with the garlic. Pour over the wine and place the rosemary sprig on top. Cover and leave to marinate in the refrigerator for 3 hours or overnight if possible.

Preheat the oven to 220°C/425°F/Gas Mark 7. Remove the lamb from the marinade, reserving the marinade. Pat the meat dry with kitchen paper and season well with salt and pepper. Place it in a small roasting tin, drizzle with the oil and roast for 15–20 minutes, depending on whether you like your meat pink or medium. Remove the lamb from the oven and leave to rest, covered with foil, in a warm place for 5 minutes.

Meanwhile, pour the reserved marinade into a small saucepan, bring to the boil over a medium heat and bubble gently for 2–3 minutes. Add the stock and redcurrant jelly and simmer, stirring, until the mixture is syrupy.

To make the Mint Sauce, chop the fresh mint leaves and mix together with the sugar in a small bowl. Add the boiling water and stir to dissolve the sugar. Add the white wine vinegar and leave to stand for 30 minutes before serving with the lamb.

Carve the lamb into cutlets and serve on warmed plates with the gravy spooned over the top. Serve the Mint Sauce separately.

Roast
Leg of Lamb

SERVES 6

- 1 leg of lamb, weighing 1.5 kg/ 3 lb 5 oz
- 6 garlic cloves, thinly sliced lengthways
- 8 fresh rosemary sprigs
- salt and pepper
- 4 tbsp olive oil

Glaze

- 4 tbsp redcurrant jelly
- 300 ml/10 fl oz rosé wine

Preheat the oven to 200°C/400°F/Gas Mark 6. Using a small knife, make small cuts all over the leg of lamb. Insert 1–2 garlic slices and 4–5 rosemary needles in each slit. Place any remaining rosemary in the base of a roasting tin. Season the lamb to taste with salt and pepper and place in the roasting tin. Pour over the oil. Cover with foil and roast for 1 hour 20 minutes.

Mix the redcurrant jelly and wine together in a small saucepan. Heat gently, stirring constantly, until combined. Bring to the boil, then reduce the heat and simmer until reduced. Remove the lamb from the oven and pour over the glaze. Return to the oven and cook uncovered for about 10 minutes, depending on how well done you like it.

Remove the lamb from the roasting tin, cover with foil and leave to rest for 15 minutes before carving and serving.

Lamb Shanks
with Roasted Onions

SERVES 4

- 4 lamb shanks, about 350 g/12 oz each
- 6 garlic cloves
- 2 tbsp virgin olive oil
- 1 tbsp fresh rosemary, very finely chopped
- 4 red onions
- 350 g/12 oz carrots, cut into thin batons
- 4 tbsp water
- salt and pepper

Preheat the oven to 180°C/350°F/Gas Mark 4. Trim off any excess fat from the lamb shanks. Using a small, sharp knife, make 6 cuts in each lamb shank. Cut the garlic cloves lengthways into 4 slices. Insert 6 garlic slices into the cuts in each lamb shank.

Put the lamb in a single layer in a roasting tin, drizzle with the oil, sprinkle with the rosemary and season to taste with pepper. Roast in the preheated oven for 45 minutes.

Wrap each of the onions in a piece of foil. Remove the roasting tin from the oven and season the lamb to taste with salt. Return to the oven and put the wrapped onions on the shelf next to it. Roast for a further 1–1¼ hours until the lamb is very tender.

Meanwhile, bring a large saucepan of water to the boil. Add the carrot batons and blanch for 1 minute. Drain and refresh in cold water.

Remove the roasting tin from the oven when the lamb is meltingly tender and transfer to a warmed serving dish. Skim off any fat from the roasting tin and put the tin over a medium heat. Add the carrots and cook, stirring, for 2 minutes, then add the water and bring to the boil. Reduce the heat and simmer, stirring constantly and scraping any sediment from the base of the tin.

Transfer the carrots and sauce to the serving dish. Remove the onions from the oven and unwrap. Cut off and discard about 1 cm/½ inch of the tops and add the onions to the serving dish. Serve immediately.

Roast Venison
with Brandy Sauce

SERVES 4

6 tbsp vegetable oil
1.7 kg/3 lb 12 oz saddle of fresh venison, trimmed
salt and pepper
fresh thyme sprigs, to garnish
freshly cooked vegetables, to serve

Brandy Sauce

1 tbsp plain flour
4 tbsp vegetable stock
175 ml/6 fl oz brandy
100 ml/3½ fl oz double cream

Preheat the oven to 180°C/350°F/Gas Mark 4.

Heat half the oil in a frying pan over a high heat. Season the venison to taste with salt and pepper, add to the pan and cook until lightly browned all over. Pour the remaining oil into a roasting pan. Add the venison, cover with foil and roast in the oven, basting occasionally, for 1½ hours, or until cooked through. Remove from the oven and transfer to a warmed serving platter. Cover with foil and set aside.

To make the sauce, stir the flour into the roasting pan over the hob and cook for 1 minute. Pour in the stock and heat it, stirring to loosen the sediment from the base. Gradually stir in the brandy and bring to the boil, then reduce the heat and simmer, stirring, for 10–15 minutes until the sauce has thickened a little. Remove from the heat and stir in the cream.

Garnish the venison with thyme and serve with the Brandy Sauce and a selection of freshly cooked vegetables.

perfect **poultry**

Roast
Chicken

SERVES 6

2.25 kg/5 lb free-range chicken
55 g/2 oz butter
2 tbsp chopped fresh lemon thyme
1 lemon, quartered
125 ml/4 fl oz white wine
salt and pepper
6 sprigs of fresh thyme, to garnish

Preheat the oven to 220°C/425°F/Gas Mark 7. Make sure the chicken is clean, wiping it inside and out using kitchen paper, and place in a roasting tin.

In a bowl, soften the butter with a fork, mix in the thyme and season well with salt and pepper. Butter the chicken all over with the herb butter, inside and out, and place the lemon pieces inside the body cavity. Pour the wine over the chicken.

Roast in the centre of the oven for 20 minutes. Reduce the temperature to 190°C/375°F/Gas Mark 5 and continue to roast for a further 1¼ hours, basting frequently. Cover with foil if the skin begins to brown too much. If the tin dries out, add a little more wine or water.

Test that the chicken is cooked by piercing the thickest part of the leg with a sharp knife or skewer and making sure the juices run clear. Remove from the oven. Remove the chicken from the roasting tin and place on a warm serving plate, cover with foil and leave to rest for 10 minutes before carving.

Place the roasting tin on the top of the stove and bubble the pan juices gently over a low heat until they have reduced and are thick and glossy. Season with salt and pepper to taste. Serve the chicken with the pan juices and scatter with the thyme sprigs.

Roast Chicken Breast Parcels
with Bread Triangles

SERVES 8

4 tbsp butter, plus extra for greasing
juice of 1 lemon
9 oz/250 g cranberries or redcurrants
1–2 tbsp brown sugar
8 skinless chicken breasts
16 lean bacon strips
4 tsp dried thyme
1/4 cup beef dripping
4 slices bread, cut into triangles
salt and pepper

Preheat the oven to 400°F/200°C. Melt the butter in a pan over a medium heat, add the lemon juice, cranberries, sugar, and salt and pepper to taste. Cook, stirring gently, for 1 minute and let cool until required.

Meanwhile, season the chicken to taste with salt and pepper. Wrap 2 bacon strips around each breast and sprinkle with thyme.

Wrap each breast in a piece of lightly greased foil and put in a roasting pan. Roast in the preheated oven for 15 minutes. Remove the foil and roast the chicken breasts for an additional 10 minutes.

Heat the dripping in a skillet over a medium–high heat. Add the bread triangles and cook on both sides until golden brown.

Put a fried bread triangle on each individual warmed serving plate and top each with a chicken breast.

Serve immediately with a spoonful of the fruit sauce.

Roast Chicken Breasts
with Sun-blush Tomato Pesto

SERVES 4

4 skinless, boneless chicken breasts, about 800 g/1 lb 12 oz in total
1 tbsp olive oil
green salad and crusty bread, to serve

Sun-blush Tomato Pesto

125 g/4½ oz sun-blush tomatoes in oil (drained weight), chopped
2 garlic cloves, crushed
6 tbsp pine kernels, lightly toasted
150 ml/5 fl oz extra-virgin olive oil

Preheat the oven to 200°C/400°F/Gas Mark 6. To make the red pesto, put the sun-blush tomatoes, garlic, 4 tablespoons of the pine kernels and the oil into a food processor and blend to a coarse paste.

Arrange the chicken in a large, ovenproof dish or roasting tin. Brush each breast with the oil, then place a tablespoon of red pesto over each breast. Using the back of a spoon, spread the pesto so that it covers the top of each breast. (This pesto recipe makes more than just the four tablespoons used here. Store the extra pesto in an airtight container in the refrigerator for up to 1 week.)

Roast the chicken in the preheated oven for 30 minutes, or until tender and the juices run clear when a skewer is inserted into the thickest part of the meat.

Sprinkle with the remaining pine nuts and serve with a green side salad and crusty bread.

Roast Turkey

SERVES 8

1 quantity of stuffing (see page 36)
1 turkey, weighing 5 kg/11 lb
55 g/2 oz butter
5 tbsp full-bodied red wine
400 ml/14 fl oz chicken stock
1 tbsp cornflour
1 tsp French mustard
1 tsp sherry vinegar
2 tsp water

To serve

bread sauce
stuffing
roast potatoes
gravy

Preheat the oven to 220°C/425°F/Gas Mark 7. Spoon the stuffing into the neck cavity of the turkey and close the flap of skin with a skewer. Put the bird in a large roasting tin and rub all over with 40 g/1½ oz of the butter. Roast in the preheated oven for 1 hour, then reduce the temperature to 180°C/350°F/Gas Mark 4 and roast for a further 2½ hours, or until tender and the juices run clear when a skewer is inserted into the thickest part of the meat. You may need to pour off the fat from the roasting tin occasionally.

When the turkey is cooked, transfer to a carving board, cover loosely with foil and leave to rest.

To make the gravy, skim off the fat from the roasting tin, then place the tin over a medium heat. Add the wine and stir, scraping the sediment from the base of the tin. Stir in the stock. Mix the cornflour, mustard, vinegar and water together in a small bowl, then stir into the tin. Bring to the boil, stirring constantly, and cook until thickened and smooth. Add the remaining butter.

Carve the turkey and serve with the gravy and all the trimmings – including bread sauce, stuffing and roast potatoes.

Roast Turkey Breast
with Cider Sauce

SERVES 8

1 boneless turkey breast roast, weighing 1 kg/2 lb 4 oz
1 tbsp sunflower or corn oil
salt and pepper

Stuffing

25 g/1 oz butter
2 shallots, finely chopped
1 celery stick, finely chopped
1 cooking apple, peeled, cored and diced
115 g/4 oz prunes, stoned and chopped
55 g/2 oz raisins
3 tbsp chicken stock
4 tbsp dry cider
1 tbsp chopped fresh parsley

Cider sauce

1 shallot, very finely chopped
300 ml/10 fl oz dry cider
125 ml/4 fl oz chicken stock
1 tsp cider vinegar

Preheat the oven to 190°C/375°F/Gas Mark 5. To make the stuffing, melt the butter in a saucepan. Add the shallots and cook, stirring occasionally, for 5 minutes. Add the celery and apple and cook for 5 minutes. Add the remaining stuffing ingredients, cover and simmer gently for 5 minutes, or until all the liquid has been absorbed. Transfer to a bowl and leave to cool.

Place the turkey roast on a chopping board and slice almost completely through, from the thin side towards the thicker side. Open out, place between 2 sheets of clingfilm and flatten with a meat mallet or rolling pin to an even thickness. Season to taste with salt. Spoon on the cooled stuffing, roll the roast around it and tie with kitchen string. Heat the oil in a roasting tin over a medium heat, add the roast and brown all over. Transfer to the oven and roast for 1 hour 10 minutes, or until cooked through and the juices run clear when the meat is pierced with a skewer.

Remove the roast from the tin and cover with foil. To make the sauce, pour off any fat from the tin and set over a medium heat. Add the shallot and half the cider and cook for 1–2 minutes, scraping any sediment from the base of the tin. Add the remaining cider, stock and vinegar and cook for 10 minutes, or until reduced and thickened. Remove and discard the string from the turkey and cut into slices. Serve with the cider sauce.

Boned & Stuffed
Roast Duckling

SERVES 6–8

1 duckling, weighing 1.8 kg/4 lb (dressed weight); ask your butcher to bone the duckling and cut off the wings at the first joint
450 g/1 lb flavoured sausage meat
1 small onion, finely chopped
1 Cox's apple, cored and finely chopped
85 g/3 oz ready-to-eat dried apricots, finely chopped
85 g/3 oz chopped walnuts
2 tbsp chopped fresh parsley
1 large or 2 smaller duck breasts, skin removed
salt and pepper

Apricot Sauce

400 g/14 oz canned apricot halves
150 ml/5 fl oz stock
125 ml/4 fl oz Marsala
1/2 tsp ground cinnamon
1/2 tsp ground ginger
salt and pepper

Wipe the duckling with kitchen paper both inside and out. Lay it skin-side down on a board and season well with salt and pepper. Mix the sausage meat, onion, apple, apricots, walnuts and parsley together. Season well with salt and pepper. Form into a large sausage shape. Lay the duck breast(s) on the whole duckling and cover with the stuffing. Wrap the whole duckling around the stuffing and carefully tuck in any leg and neck flaps.

Preheat the oven to 190°C/375°F/Gas Mark 5. Sew the duckling up the back and across both ends with fine string. Try to use one piece of string so that you can remove it in one go. Mould the duckling into a good shape and place, sewn-side down, on a wire rack over a roasting tin.

Roast in the oven for 1½–2 hours, basting occasionally. Pour off some of the fat in the tin. When it is cooked, the duckling should be golden brown and the skin crisp.

Purée the apricots, with their syrup, in a blender or food processor. Pour into a saucepan, add the stock, Marsala, cinnamon and ginger and season with salt and pepper. Stir over a low heat, then simmer for 2–3 minutes.

Carve the duckling into thick slices at the table and serve with warm Apricot Sauce.

Roast Duck Breasts
with Onion Marmalade

SERVES 4

4 duck breasts, about 185 g/ 6½ oz each
2 tbsp runny honey
salt and pepper
freshly cooked vegetables, to serve

Onion Marmalade

50 g/1¾ oz butter
2 ripe but firm pears, peeled, cored and sliced
6 onions, sliced
2 tbsp dark chestnut honey
2 pieces stem ginger
2 tbsp stem ginger syrup

Preheat the oven to 200°C/400°F/Gas Mark 6.

To make the marmalade, melt the butter in a saucepan over a medium–high heat, add the pears and onions and cook, stirring occasionally, for 10 minutes, or until soft and golden.

Add the honey, stem ginger and ginger syrup and bubble gently for 15–20 minutes until the mixture is sticky and caramelized. Season to taste with salt and pepper. Keep warm until needed.

Meanwhile, heat a frying pan over a medium–high heat until hot. Add the duck breasts, skin-side down, to the hot frying pan. There is no need to add any fat; the breasts will release plenty as they cook. Cook for 2–3 minutes until golden brown. Turn the breasts over and cook for a further 2–3 minutes. Transfer the breasts to a roasting dish, brush with the honey and season to taste with salt and pepper. Roast in the preheated oven for 12 minutes. Remove from the oven and leave to rest in a warm place for 5 minutes.

To serve, cut each duck breast into slices and fan out on each of four warmed dinner plates. Serve immediately with the Onion Marmalade and freshly cooked vegetables.

Roast Goose
with Cinnamon Red Cabbage

SERVES 6

1 oven-ready goose, weighing about 4.5 kg/10 lb
2 onions, quartered
2 bay leaves
1 bunch fresh thyme
salt and pepper

Cinnamon Red Cabbage

3 tbsp olive oil
1 large onion, sliced
1 red cabbage, shredded
1 large cooking apple, peeled, cored and chopped
3 tbsp raisins
300 ml/10 fl oz red wine
50 ml/2 fl oz red wine vinegar
2 tsp caster sugar, or to taste
1 cinnamon stick

Preheat the oven to 200°C/400°F/Gas Mark 6.

Cut away any excess fat from the tail area of the goose. Season the goose cavity to taste with salt and pepper and push in the onion quarters, bay leaves and thyme, reserving a few sprigs for the garnish. Put the goose on a rack set over a roasting tin and prick the skin all over with a skewer. Season the outside of the goose to taste with salt and pepper. Roast in the preheated oven for 15 minutes per 450 g/1 lb, plus an extra 15 minutes. Remove from the oven, cover loosely with foil and leave to rest for 15 minutes before carving.

While the goose is roasting, prepare the red cabbage. Heat the oil in a large frying pan over a medium heat, add the onion and cook, stirring frequently, for 3–4 minutes until softened but not coloured. Add all the remaining ingredients, cover and cook for 30–40 minutes until the cabbage is tender and the liquid has reduced. Remove the cinnamon stick before serving.

Carve the goose and serve in slices, accompanied by the red cabbage and garnished with the reserved thyme.

fantastic **fish**

Roasted
Salmon

SERVES 4

6 tbsp extra virgin olive oil
1 onion, sliced
1 leek, sliced
juice of ½ lemon
2 tbsp chopped fresh parsley
2 tbsp chopped fresh dill
500 g/1 lb 2 oz salmon fillets
salt and pepper
freshly cooked baby spinach leaves, to serve

To garnish

lemon slices
fresh dill sprigs

Preheat the oven to 200°C/400°F/Gas Mark 6.

Heat 1 tablespoon of the oil in a frying pan over a medium heat. Add the onion and leek and cook, stirring occasionally, for 4 minutes, or until slightly softened.

Meanwhile, put the remaining oil in a small bowl with the lemon juice and herbs and season to taste with salt and pepper. Stir together well. Rinse the fish under cold running water, then pat dry with kitchen paper. Arrange the fish in a shallow ovenproof dish.

Remove the frying pan from the heat and spread the onion and leek over the fish. Pour the oil mixture over the top, making sure that everything is well coated. Roast in the centre of the preheated oven for 10 minutes, or until the fish is cooked through.

Arrange the cooked spinach on serving plates. Remove the fish and vegetables from the oven and arrange beside the spinach. Garnish with lemon slices and sprigs of dill. Serve immediately.

Roast Monkfish
with Romesco Sauce

SERVES 4–6

- 1 monkfish tail, about 900 g/ 2 lb, membrane removed
- 2–3 slices serrano ham
- olive oil, for brushing
- salt and pepper

Romesco Sauce

- 1 red pepper, halved and deseeded
- 4 garlic cloves, unpeeled
- 2 tomatoes, halved
- 125 ml/4 fl oz olive oil
- 1 slice white bread, diced
- 4 tbsp blanched almonds
- 1 fresh red chilli, deseeded and chopped
- 2 shallots, chopped
- 1 tsp paprika
- 2 tbsp red wine vinegar
- 2 tsp sugar
- 1 tbsp water

Preheat the oven to 220°C/425°F/Gas Mark 7. For the sauce, put the pepper, garlic and tomatoes in a roasting tin and toss with 1 tablespoon of the oil. Roast in the oven for 20–25 minutes, then remove from the oven, cover with a tea towel and set aside for 10 minutes. Peel off the skins and place the vegetables in a food processor.

Heat 1 tablespoon of the remaining oil in a frying pan. Add the bread cubes and almonds and cook over a low heat, stirring frequently, until golden. Remove with a slotted spoon and drain on kitchen paper. Add the chilli, shallots and paprika to the frying pan and cook, stirring occasionally, for 5 minutes.

Transfer the bread and chilli mixtures to the food processor, add the vinegar, sugar and water and process to a paste. With the motor running, add the remaining oil through the feeder tube. Set aside. Reduce the oven temperature to 200°C/400°F/Gas Mark 6. Rinse the monkfish tail and pat it dry. Wrap the ham around the monkfish and brush lightly with oil. Season to taste with salt and pepper. Put the fish on a baking sheet.

Roast the monkfish in the oven for 20 minutes until the flesh is opaque and flakes easily. Test by lifting off the ham along the central bone and cut a small amount of the flesh away from the bone to see if it flakes. Cut through the ham to remove the central bone and produce 2 thick fillets. Cut each fillet into 2 or 3 pieces and arrange on plates with a spoonful of Romesco Sauce. Serve immediately.

Garlic-Crusted
Roast Haddock

SERVES 4

900 g/2 lb floury potatoes
125 ml/4 fl oz milk
55 g/2 oz butter
4 haddock fillets, about 225 g/8 oz each
1 tbsp sunflower oil
4 garlic cloves, finely chopped
salt and pepper
2 tbsp chopped fresh parsley, to garnish

Preheat the oven to 230°C/450°F/Gas Mark 8. Cut the potatoes into chunks and cook in a saucepan of lightly salted water for 15 minutes, or until tender. Drain well. Mash in the saucepan until smooth. Set over a low heat and beat in the milk, butter and salt and pepper to taste.

Put the haddock fillets in a roasting tin and brush the fish with the oil. Sprinkle the garlic on top, add salt and pepper to taste, then spread with the mashed potatoes. Roast in the oven for 8–10 minutes, or until the fish is just tender.

Meanwhile, preheat the grill. Transfer the fish to the grill and cook for about 2 minutes, or until golden brown. Sprinkle with the chopped parsley and serve immediately.

Italian Cod

SERVES 4

- 25 g/1 oz butter
- 50 g/1¾ oz fresh wholemeal breadcrumbs
- 25 g/1 oz chopped walnuts
- grated rind and juice of 2 lemons
- 2 fresh rosemary sprigs, stalks removed
- 2 tbsp chopped fresh parsley
- 4 cod fillets, about 150 g/5½ oz each
- 1 garlic clove, crushed
- 1 small fresh red chilli, diced
- 3 tbsp walnut oil
- mixed salad leaves, to serve

Preheat the oven to 200°C/400°F/Gas Mark 6.

Melt the butter in a large saucepan over a low heat, stirring constantly. Remove the pan from the heat and add the breadcrumbs, walnuts, the rind and juice of 1 lemon, half the rosemary and half the parsley, stirring to mix.

Press the breadcrumb mixture over the top of the cod fillets. Place the cod fillets in a shallow foil-lined roasting tin. Roast the fish in the oven for 25–30 minutes.

Mix the garlic, the remaining lemon rind and juice, rosemary, parsley and the chilli together in a bowl. Beat in the oil and mix to combine. Drizzle the dressing over the cod steaks as soon as they are cooked.

Transfer the fish to warmed serving plates and serve immediately with salad leaves.

Fish Roasted
with Lime

SERVES 4

1 kg/2 lb 4 oz white fish fillets, such as bass, plaice or cod
1 lime, halved
3 tbsp extra virgin olive oil
1 large onion, finely chopped
3 garlic cloves, finely chopped
2–3 pickled jalapeño chillies (jalapeños en escabeche), chopped
6–8 tbsp chopped fresh coriander
salt and pepper
lemon and lime wedges, to serve

Preheat the oven to 180°C/350°F/Gas Mark 4.

Place the fish fillets in a non-metallic bowl and season to taste with salt and pepper. Squeeze the juice from the lime halves over the fish. Heat the oil in a frying pan. Add the onion and garlic and cook, stirring frequently, for 2 minutes, or until softened. Remove the frying pan from the heat.

Place a third of the onion mixture and a little of the chillies and coriander in the base of a shallow ovenproof dish or roasting tin. Arrange the fish on top. Top with the remaining onion mixture, chillies and coriander.

Roast in the oven for 15–20 minutes, or until the fish has become slightly opaque and firm to the touch. Serve immediately, with lemon and lime wedges for squeezing over the fish.

Roast
Seafood

SERVES 4

600 g/1 lb 5 oz new potatoes
3 red onions, cut into wedges
2 courgettes, cut into chunks
8 garlic cloves, peeled but left whole
2 lemons, cut into wedges
4 fresh rosemary sprigs
4 tbsp olive oil
350 g/12 oz unpeeled raw prawns
2 small raw squid, cut into rings
4 tomatoes, quartered

Preheat the oven to 200°C/400°F/Gas Mark 6. Scrub the potatoes to remove any dirt. Cut any large potatoes in half. Parboil the potatoes in a saucepan of boiling water for 10–15 minutes. Place the potatoes in a large roasting tin together with the onions, courgettes, garlic, lemons and rosemary sprigs.

Pour over the oil and toss to coat all the vegetables in it. Roast in the oven for 30 minutes, turning occasionally, until the potatoes are tender.

Once the potatoes are tender, add the prawns, squid and tomatoes, tossing to coat them in the oil, and roast for 10 minutes. All the vegetables should be cooked through and slightly charred for full flavour.

Transfer the roast seafood and vegetables to warmed serving plates and serve hot.

Flounder
for Two

SERVES 2

150 ml/5 fl oz olive oil
375 g/13 oz waxy potatoes, peeled and thinly sliced
1 fennel bulb, thinly sliced
2 large tomatoes, grilled, peeled, deseeded and chopped
2 shallots, sliced
1–2 whole flounders, cleaned, about 1.3 kg/3 lb
4 tbsp dry white wine
2 tbsp finely chopped fresh parsley
salt and pepper
lemon wedges, to serve

Preheat the oven to 200°C/400°F/Gas Mark 6. Spread 4 tablespoons of the oil over the base of a shallow roasting tin large enough to hold the flounder. Arrange the potatoes in a single layer, then top with the fennel, tomatoes and shallots. Season to taste with salt and pepper. Drizzle with a further 4 tablespoons of the oil. Roast the vegetables in the preheated oven for 30 minutes.

Season the fish to taste with salt and pepper and put on top of the vegetables. Sprinkle with the wine and the remaining oil.

Return the roasting tin to the oven and roast the fish, uncovered, for 20 minutes, or until the flesh flakes easily.

Transfer the vegetables to 2 serving plates and place the fish on top. Serve immediately, accompanied by the lemon wedges for squeezing over.

Mussels with Herb & *Garlic Butter*

SERVES 8

800 g/1 lb 12 oz live mussels, cleaned
splash of dry white wine
1 bay leaf
85 g/3 oz butter
35 g/1¼ oz fresh white or brown breadcrumbs
4 tbsp chopped fresh flat-leaf parsley, plus extra sprigs to garnish
2 tbsp snipped fresh chives
2 garlic cloves, finely chopped
salt and pepper
lemon wedges, to serve

Preheat the oven to 230°C/450°F/Gas Mark 8.

Put the mussels in a large saucepan and add the wine and bay leaf. Cook, covered, over a high heat, shaking the saucepan occasionally, for 3–4 minutes, or until the mussels have opened. Discard any that remain closed. Strain the mussels.

Shell the mussels, reserving one half of each shell. Arrange the mussels, in their half shells, in a large, shallow, ovenproof serving dish.

Melt the butter in a small saucepan and pour into a small bowl. Add the breadcrumbs, parsley, chives, garlic, and salt and pepper to taste, and mix together well. Leave until the butter has set slightly. Using your fingers or 2 teaspoons, take a large pinch of the mixture and use to fill each mussel shell, pressing it down well.

Bake the mussels in the preheated oven for 10 minutes, or until hot. Serve immediately, garnished with the parsley sprigs, accompanied by the lemon wedges for squeezing over.

vegetable **magic**

Perfect
Roast Potatoes

SERVES 6

1.3 kg/3 lb large floury potatoes, such as King Edwards, Maris Piper or Desirée, peeled and cut into even-sized chunks
3 tbsp dripping, goose fat, duck fat or olive oil
salt

Preheat the oven to 220°C/425°F/Gas Mark 7.

Cook the potatoes in a large saucepan of lightly salted boiling water over a medium heat, covered, for 5–7 minutes. They will still be firm. Remove from the heat. Meanwhile, add the fat to a roasting tin and place in the hot oven.

Drain the potatoes well and return them to the saucepan. Cover with the lid and firmly shake the pan so that the surface of the potatoes is slightly roughened to help give a much crisper texture.

Remove the roasting tin from the oven and carefully tip the potatoes into the hot fat. Baste them to ensure that they are all coated with it.

Roast the potatoes at the top of the oven for 45–50 minutes until they are browned all over and thoroughly crisp. Turn the potatoes only once during the process or the crunchy edges will be destroyed. Baste again.

Using a slotted spoon, carefully transfer the potatoes from the roasting tin into a warmed serving dish. Sprinkle with a little salt and serve immediately. Any leftovers (although this is most unlikely) are delicious cold.

Chilli Roast
Potatoes

SERVES 4

500 g/1 lb 2 oz small new potatoes, scrubbed
150 ml/5 fl oz vegetable oil
1 tsp chilli powder
½ tsp caraway seeds
1 tsp salt

Preheat the oven to 200°C/400°F/Gas Mark 6. Cook the potatoes in a large saucepan of boiling water for 10 minutes, then drain thoroughly.

Meanwhile, pour a little of the oil into a shallow roasting tin to coat the base. Heat the oil in the oven for 10 minutes, then remove the tin from the oven. Add the potatoes and brush them with the hot oil.

Mix the chilli powder, caraway seeds and salt together in a small bowl, then sprinkle the mixture evenly over the potatoes, turning them to coat. Add the remaining oil to the tin and return to the oven to roast for 15 minutes, or until the potatoes are cooked through and golden brown.

Using a slotted spoon, remove the potatoes from the tin, draining well, transfer to a large warmed serving dish and serve immediately.

Roast Garlic
Mashed Potatoes

SERVES 4

2 whole garlic bulbs
1 tbsp olive oil
900 g/2 lb floury potatoes, peeled
125 ml/4 fl oz milk
55 g/2 oz butter
salt and pepper

Preheat the oven to 180°C/350°F/Gas Mark 4.

Separate the garlic cloves, place on a large piece of foil and drizzle with the oil. Wrap the garlic in the foil and roast in the oven for about 1 hour, or until very tender. Leave to cool slightly.

Twenty minutes before the end of the cooking time, cut the potatoes into chunks, then cook in a saucepan of lightly salted boiling water for 15 minutes, or until tender.

Meanwhile, squeeze the cooled garlic cloves out of their skins and push through a sieve into a saucepan. Add the milk, butter and salt and pepper to taste and heat gently until the butter has melted.

Drain the cooked potatoes, then mash in the saucepan until smooth. Pour in the garlic mixture and heat gently, stirring, until the ingredients are combined. Serve hot.

Roast Root *Vegetables*

SERVES 4–6

3 parsnips, cut into 5-cm/2-inch chunks
4 baby turnips, quartered
3 carrots, cut into 5-cm/2-inch chunks
450 g/1 lb butternut squash, peeled and cut into 5-cm/2-inch chunks
450 g/1 lb sweet potatoes, peeled and cut into 5-cm/2-inch chunks
2 garlic cloves, finely chopped
2 tbsp chopped fresh rosemary
2 tbsp chopped fresh thyme
2 tsp chopped fresh sage
3 tbsp olive oil
salt and pepper
2 tbsp chopped fresh mixed herbs, such as parsley, thyme and mint, to garnish

Preheat the oven to 220°C/425°F/Gas Mark 7.

Arrange all the vegetables in a single layer in a large roasting tin. Scatter over the garlic and the herbs. Pour over the oil and season well with salt and pepper.

Toss all the ingredients together until they are well mixed and coated with the oil (you can leave them to marinate at this stage to allow the flavours to be absorbed).

Roast the vegetables at the top of the oven for 50–60 minutes until they are cooked and nicely browned. Turn the vegetables over halfway through the cooking time.

Serve with a good handful of fresh herbs scattered on top and a final sprinkling of salt and pepper to taste.

Roast
Onions

SERVES 4

8 large onions, peeled but left whole
3 tbsp olive oil
55 g/2 oz butter
2 tsp chopped fresh thyme
200 g/7 oz Cheddar or Lancashire cheese, grated
salt and pepper

To serve

salad
warm crusty bread

Preheat the oven to 180°C/350°F/Gas Mark 4.

Cut a cross down through the top of each onion towards the root, without cutting all the way through. Place the onions in a roasting tin and drizzle over the oil.

Press a little of the butter into the open crosses, sprinkle with the thyme and season to taste with salt and pepper. Cover with foil and roast in the oven for 40–45 minutes.

Remove the tin from the oven, take off and discard the foil and baste the onions with the pan juices. Return to the oven and cook for a further 15 minutes, uncovered, to allow the onions to brown.

Take the onions out of the oven and scatter the grated cheese over them. Return them to the oven for a few minutes so that the cheese starts to melt.

Serve immediately with some salad and lots of warm crusty bread.

Roast Summer *Vegetables*

SERVES 4

- 2 tbsp olive oil
- 1 fennel bulb
- 2 red onions
- 2 beef tomatoes
- 1 aubergine
- 2 courgettes
- 1 yellow pepper
- 1 red pepper
- 1 orange pepper
- 4 garlic cloves, peeled but left whole
- 4 fresh rosemary sprigs
- pepper
- crusty bread, to serve (optional)

Preheat the oven to 200°C/400°F/Gas Mark 6.

Brush a large ovenproof dish with a little of the oil. Prepare the vegetables. Cut the fennel bulb, red onions and tomatoes into wedges. Slice the aubergine and courgettes thickly, then deseed all the peppers and cut into chunks. Arrange the vegetables in the dish and tuck the garlic cloves and rosemary sprigs among them. Drizzle with the remaining oil and season to taste with pepper.

Roast the vegetables in the oven for 10 minutes. Remove the dish from the oven and turn the vegetables over using a slotted spoon. Return the dish to the oven and roast for a further 10–15 minutes, or until the vegetables are tender and beginning to turn golden brown.

Serve the vegetables straight from the dish or transfer them to a warmed serving plate. For a vegetarian main course, serve with crusty bread, if you like.

Crispy Roast *Asparagus*

SERVES 4

450 g/1 lb asparagus spears

2 tbsp extra virgin olive oil

1 tsp coarse sea salt

1 tbsp freshly grated Parmesan cheese, to serve

Preheat the oven to 200°C/400°F/Gas Mark 6.

Choose asparagus spears of similar widths. Trim the base of the spears so that all the stems are approximately the same length.

Arrange the asparagus in a single layer on a baking sheet. Drizzle with the oil and sprinkle with the salt.

Place the baking sheet in the oven and roast the asparagus for 10–15 minutes, turning the spears once. Remove from the oven and transfer to a warmed dish. Serve immediately, sprinkled with grated Parmesan cheese.

Lemon Butter Leeks
with Poor Man's Parmesan

SERVES 6

9 chubby leeks, trimmed and halved lengthways
juice and finely grated rind of 1 unwaxed lemon
1 tsp caster sugar
75 g/2¾ oz butter
5 tbsp mascarpone cheese
salt and pepper

Poor Man's Parmesan

30 g/1 oz butter
50 g/1¾ fresh ciabatta crumbs

Preheat the oven to 190°C/375°F/Gas Mark 5.

Lay the halved leeks out in an even layer in an ovenproof dish. Drizzle over the lemon juice and scatter over the lemon rind, then evenly sprinkle over the sugar. Season to taste with pepper and evenly dot with the butter. Bake in the preheated oven for 15 minutes, or until the leeks are beginning to soften and caramelize.

Meanwhile, make the Poor Man's Parmesan. Melt the butter in a frying pan over a medium heat, add the ciabatta crumbs and cook, stirring, until crisp and golden. Season with a little salt and pepper and set aside.

Remove the leeks from the oven and evenly dot with the mascarpone cheese. Scatter the Poor Man's Parmesan over the leeks and return to the oven. Bake for a further 5 minutes, or until the mascarpone has melted and the crumbs are hot and crisp. Serve immediately.